be

HAPPY

be HAPPY

His Holiness the
Dalai Lama

Copyright © The Dalai Lama Foundation 2018, 2019

First published in 2018 as *Happiness* by Penguin Books,
Penguin Random House India. ISBN 9780143442998

Hampton Roads Publishing Company, Inc.
Charlottesville, VA 22906
Distributed by Red Wheel/Weiser, LLC

www.redwheelweiser.com
Cover and text design by Kathryn Sky-Peck
Graphic image of the Dalai Lama from *www.vectorportal.com*

ISBN: 978-1-64297-003-6
Library of Congress Cataloging-in-Publication Data
available on request.

Printed in Canada
FR
10 9 8 7 6 5 4 3 2 1

Publisher's note:

Everyone wants to be happy. However, just the "wanting" of that happiness can cause us so much suffering. What is happiness? Where do we find it? Is it something we create or something we deserve? How do we go about achieving it?

This little volume is a road map for discovering your path to happiness, joy, and a sense of purpose. The Dalai Lama teaches that each of us is responsible for our own happiness and that happiness is always within our reach—both individually and collectively.

In this intimate discussion, with his characteristic wisdom, humor, and kindness, His Holiness the Dalai Lama breaks down what it means to be happy and shows us that how we think, behave, and sensually experience the world ultimately impacts how we experience—and create—happiness.

In this little book, His Holiness the Dalai Lama tells us: "Be happy."

Just *be*.

Herein are the keys to *being* happy. If you desire to attain happiness, you must understand that the journey begins with you. It is only then that you can reach out and touch the lives of others and change society.

With his characteristic down-to-earth approach to the Buddhist path, His Holiness the Dalai Lama has often observed of himself that his informal speaking style "complements my broken English." This volume has been edited to keep alive his voice and its unique flavor.

.

HAPPINESS

Dear brothers and sisters, I am very happy to have this opportunity to talk to you. Whenever I give a talk, I always have this feeling that we human beings are all the same—mentally, emotionally, and physically.

Everyone wants a happy life. Nobody wakes up in the morning wishing for more trouble that day. However, emotional trouble is essentially our own creation.

"EMOTIONAL TROUBLE

—UNHAPPINESS—

IS ESSENTIALLY

OUR OWN CREATION."

I think this is largely due to two things: The first reason is our lack of knowledge of reality (essentially because we are absent a holistic view); the second reason is a self-centered attitude.

These two things—lack of knowledge and a self-centered attitude—create unnecessary problems.

We can't blame our problems on anybody or anything else. Ultimately, we have to realize that the cause of these problems lies within ourselves.

So how do we deal with them?

We deal with them not through prayer, not through money, not through power, but through understanding and awareness—what we may call wisdom.

Happiness. Everyone, including animals, wants less mental disturbance. But before talking about the source of happiness, it might be useful to know something about the system of our minds.

Happiness, which we may think of as just an emotion, is a product of our minds. Usually people are under the impression that the mind is independent, absolute.

"LACK OF KNOWLEDGE AND
A SELF-CENTERED ATTITUDE
CREATE UNNECESSARY
PROBLEMS."

"HAPPINESS,

WHICH WE MAY THINK OF AS

JUST AN EMOTION,

IS A PRODUCT OF

OUR MINDS."

Science, too, is not yet clear about the distinction between the sensorial mind and consciousness. It is important to make that distinction.

When people seek pleasurable experiences, they rely mainly on the sensorial level to attain that pleasure—watching something beautiful, listening to music, tasting or smelling something. This includes tactile pleasures, including sex. And just like pleasure, pain is also part of our experiences.

Positive experiences are mainly registered at the sensorial level; they are the products of our five senses. But these sensorial experiences are temporary. The object of beauty you behold or the beautiful music you hear is gone the moment you stop seeing or hearing it.

In contrast, if you develop your pleasurable, positive experiences at a *mental level*, the experience of pleasure lasts longer.

You can experience a feeling of calm through your five senses—by being in a calming environment for example. Or you can experience a feeling of calm in your mind. So a disturbing noise at the

"HAPPINESS IS A
SENSE OF FULFILLMENT
AT THE MENTAL LEVEL
OF CONSCIOUSNESS."

sensorial level will not affect this basic calmness. Even the pain of physical illness can be subdued in this state.

On the other hand, no sensorial pleasure can be had if the basic mental state is one of fear, anxiety, and stress.

Obviously, mental-level experiences are more important than sensorial ones.

It is important to understand that mental-level happiness need not be about pleasure. It's about mental satisfaction or fulfilment.

"MENTAL-LEVEL HAPPINESS

NEED NOT BE

ABOUT PLEASURE."

Even physical suffering and pain can bring deep satisfaction at the mental level.

Happiness mainly refers to this feeling at the level of consciousness.

All major religious traditions try to bring about calmness, peacefulness, and positivity at the mental level. Faith is not at the sensorial level. It is the sixth consciousness.

Of course, the sensorial level helps in attaining mental satisfaction; for example, seeing the image of the Buddha or a god or listening to prayers.

However, the real effect is due to faith. The practice of love and compassion—and with them, forgiveness, tolerance, and contentment—operates at the level of mental consciousness.

Cause and Effect

There are nontheistic religious traditions—such as Sankhya, a 3,000-year-old Indian tradition, as well as Jainism and Buddhism—that do not talk about a creator but believe instead in the law of causality, or the law of cause and effect.

Everybody in this country is familiar with the concept of karma: cause and effect. It means action.

Any action—whether physical, verbal, or mental—arising out of any positive emotion or sincere motivation, like

"ANY ACTION

ARISING OUT OF

POSITIVE EMOTION

IS GOOD KARMA."

compassion and forgiveness, is positive or good karma.

When the motivation is good, when there's a sense of concern for others' well-being, when an action benefits others as well as oneself, then the action is considered positive. Otherwise, there's no absolute "positive" or "negative."

For example, anger, hatred, and suspicion are considered negative. But suspicion may be positive or negative, since suspicion leads us to action.

"Negative" is a concept that merely means that which is uncomfortable to oneself or to others. Any such motivation will lead to physical, verbal, or mental action that can produce negative karma.

Experiences of pleasure, pain, and the actions that cause them constitute the law of causality.

Both Jainism and Buddhism may have different approaches to many aspects of life, but the fundamental goals are the same: to enhance our ability to love and forgive and to be compassionate in day-to-day life.

"THE FUNDAMENTAL GOALS
ARE TO ENHANCE OUR ABILITY
TO LOVE AND FORGIVE
AND TO BE COMPASSIONATE
IN DAY-TO-DAY LIFE."

Theistic religions use the concept of god or the creator. On the other hand, nontheistic traditions use the concept of the law of causality. They believe that if you are good to others, you will benefit, and if you harm others, you will suffer negative consequences.

Compassion and Happiness

Interestingly, there is also another way to look at karma. Without touching upon the mysterious aspects of religions, but only by looking at the obvious mundane ones, we can educate people about compassion and how it can lead to happiness. Let's look at an example from the animal world.

First, biologically, all social animals show a sense of responsibility toward their group. The reality is that individual survival and well-being depend upon the welfare of the group. Because

"WE CAN EDUCATE PEOPLE

ABOUT COMPASSION AND

HOW IT CAN LEAD

TO HAPPINESS."

""NO INDIVIDUAL

CAN SURVIVE ALONE,

LET ALONE BE HAPPY.""

of this reality, every individual has a sense of community.

No matter how powerful, no individual can survive alone, let alone be happy. His very survival depends on the rest of his community. That's a fact. Because of that, there must be some emotion that produces affection and brings community members close to each other.

While compassion brings a community closer, anger does the opposite. Anger and fear—which push an individual away from his community—are harmful to survival.

Of course, fear can be positive, too—as a defense against danger, as it produces caution. So at the emotional level, we are wired to protect ourselves and our interests and to expel the opposite.

Affection and compassion are part of our psyche, intended to help us survive.

It is the same with dogs, cats, and birds. Humans, however, have this marvellous *intelligence*. On the basis of our biological and emotional potential, we should use our intelligence for long-term interests.

With a wider perspective of interest, we can then increase our compassion, toward which we are naturally inclined.

The biological wiring for love and compassion is limited, biased, and often accompanied by hatred and suspicion. Nevertheless, if we are trained to use it with intelligence, reason, and logic for a longer term and with a broader perspective, it could certainly become unbiased.

We develop a biological compassion toward a friend who favors us and hatred toward an enemy who does not

"AFFECTION AND COMPASSION
ARE PART OF OUR PSYCHE,
INTENDED TO HELP US SURVIVE."

favor us. If your friend has a good attitude toward you, you love him.

On the other hand, if this person is your antagonist, his attitude is harmful to you. Therefore, you hate him.

Now use your intelligence. Irrespective of whether someone is your friend or an enemy, that person is still a part of your community. Your life depends on the community. Not everyone is necessarily your friend. However, you need one another for survival.

Us and Them

An old way of thinking was "us" and "them," with a solid barrier in between. "We" don't care about "them." In ancient times, each nation was more or less independent. Today, everything is more global and interdependent. So that feeling of"us" versus "them" should ideally be becoming outdated.

For our global survival, we must consider the rest of the world and humanity as part of "us," because our best interests depend on everyone else's. There's no relevance here of personal attitude.

"FOR OUR GLOBAL SURVIVAL,

WE MUST CONSIDER

THE REST OF HUMANITY

AS PART OF 'US'."

Using this reasoning, we can extend our genuine sense of concern and well-being to others because they are a part of our community. We can orient ourselves toward them as brothers and sisters of our community; we can extend our love and compassion to them.

An animal can't do that intellectually. We human beings can use our intelligence to do that. We have the potential to develop that level of compassion.

That is unbiased, genuine compassion.

It is important to make a distinction here. If your so-called adversary creates a problem for you, you may take an appropriate countermeasure as far as action is concerned. But as a human being, you can still continue to be compassionate and have a sense of concern for his well-being.

In fact, out of genuine concern for his well-being, if you let his wrongdoings go unchecked, ultimately he will suffer. So take that countermeasure in order to stop him from doing anything wrong.

While it's a countermeasure, it is also an act of compassion. So this is a way of

"HAPPINESS MEANS A PEACEFUL MIND, WHICH IS DEVOID OF STRESS, ANXIETY, OR FEAR. . . .

. . . ON ONE LEVEL, YOU CAN SEE

NEGATIVE THINGS, BUT AT A DEEPER

LEVEL, YOU CAN STILL BE CALM."

training our mind, not through meditation but by utilizing our intelligence.

Once we develop this mental attitude, based on reason and open-mindedness, we can be happy. Here happiness means a peaceful mind, which is devoid of stress, anxiety, or fear.

On one level, you can see negative things, but at a deeper level, you can still be calm, irrespective of whether you are a believer or a nonbeliever.

Science speaks of a close link between a healthy body and a healthy mind. An agitated mind over a long period of time can be very harmful to one's physical well-being. A calm, healthy mind is extremely beneficial for physical health. Fear, anger, and hatred actually eat into our immune system.

On the other hand, a less stressful mind is extremely helpful in maintaining good physical health.

The Inner Door

I would like to share with you an incident that happened in New York City during a meeting of medical scientists and other people.

One of the scientists mentioned that according to his findings, people who express themselves frequently using "I," "me," and "mine" have a greater risk of having heart attacks. These people are too self-centered; such an attitude makes even a small problem unbearable.

Once you open your heart to others' well-being, which I call the opening of your inner door, you can communicate with other people easily. This will help you make more friends, reduce feelings of loneliness, and develop feelings of compassion, which reduces anxiety. And that is useful for our health. After all, we are social animals and such an attitude goes well with our reality.

Generally, people stress the importance of education. They are right. Many problems arise due to lack of knowledge and ignorance. Education can equip you to develop a broader,

"OPEN YOUR HEART TO OTHERS' WELL-BEING, WHICH I CALL OPENING YOUR INNER DOOR."

more comprehensive, and more holistic perspective. Education should reduce the gap between appearance and reality. Everybody understands the importance of education.

On the basis of scientific findings, we know that positive emotions are important for our health, for a happy individual, a happy family, and a happy community. This I consider the real art of happiness. I've learned this through personal experience.

I'm eighty-three years old now. I lost my freedom at the early age of sixteen.

"POSITIVE EMOTIONS ARE
IMPORTANT
FOR OUR HEALTH, FOR A HAPPY
INDIVIDUAL, A HAPPY FAMILY, AND A
HAPPY COMMUNITY. . . .

. . . THIS I CONSIDER THE

REAL ART OF HAPPINESS. "

At the age of twenty-four, I became a refugee. I was a stateless, homeless individual. While I lost a small home in Tibet, I found a big home in India.

Throughout my life, I have gone through turbulence, but my mind continues to remain peaceful—not through dullness, I hope.

Moreover, I feel that my mind is quite sharp. When I engage with famous scientists, my knowledge is almost zero compared to theirs, but we logically analyze every single point. That helps sharpen the mind. So I hope my mind is not that dull.

However, during these turbulent times, my mind is calm. The immediate result is that my health is good except that an important organ, the gallbladder, is gone. So while this human body looks normal, there's one important organ missing. Basically my health is very good.

My mental state, I think, is what makes the difference. My physician friends tell me my physical condition is not like that of a eighty-plus man and that I seem ten years younger.

"DURING THESE

TURBULENT TIMES,

MY MIND IS CALM."

Some introduce me as a reincarnation of the Bodhisattva, but I know I am no higher being or anyone like that.

I know my own mind. I can read my own mind. I am a human being who utilizes his intelligence properly. The result is a mentally happy, physically healthy human being.

Everybody has the same potential. The only thing is whether they pay attention or not, whether they have sufficient awareness or not; that is the point. Otherwise, all of us have the same potential.

"TO BE HAPPY,

YOU MUST KNOW

YOUR OWN MIND."

I think ancient Indian treasures have detailed knowledge of human emotions, of the human mind. So, naturally, regardless of whether it is Jainism, Buddhism, or Hinduism, all religions have a common practice of samadhan and vipassana, both of which involve mental training.

Since these traditions follow these practices, they follow a map of the mind. I think that needs to be taught more. It should be part of an academic subject.

Western psychology is very limited. The world of the mind is so vast; it is very

"EVERYBODY

HAS THE SAME POTENTIAL

FOR HAPPINESS. . . .

. . . THE ONLY THING IS

WHETHER WE PAY ATTENTION

AND HAVE SUFFICIENT

AWARENESS."

important to know the system, to know different minds and how they develop and work.

For medical knowledge, you need to know the body and how it works. For mental awareness, too, we need to study the system of the mind as an academic subject and not as a religious subject.

If that knowledge is used to attain heaven (or hell!) in the afterlife, it becomes a religious thing. If it's used to attain well-being in this life, it has nothing to do with religion.

I often tease my Indian friends. When one worships one's god or goddess every day with incense sticks and flowers, and recites Sanskrit shlokas without knowing their meanings, it's of no use.

We must pay more attention and study this rich ancient Indian thought. India is a religious nation.

I often say that religious faith and unjust actions cannot go together. There is no third choice. There are only two choices: to be religious-minded, carrying on an honest, just, truthful life, or to lead a corrupt life, denying god, denying karma, and just seeking money and power.

Thus, the "third choice"—being both religious and corrupt—is a big contradiction. Pray to Shiva, Ganesha, and, in the meantime, have no hesitation in being corrupt.

Whether it is made up of believers or nonbelievers, society should be clean, transparent; when everybody is happy, a nation can be built more rapidly.

Where there is a lot of corruption and injustice, poor people suffer the most.

"DEVELOPING POSITIVE EMOTIONS IS THE REAL ART OF HAPPINESS."

"WHEN EVERYBODY

IS HAPPY,

A NATION CAN BE BUILT

MORE RAPIDLY."

From the viewpoint of national interest, India is the second most populated nation and has shown great stability in the last sixty years because of its vibrant democracy and rule of law.

The citizens of this country should think about how to build a healthy nation.

Each individual has a moral responsibility to build India in a more healthy way. Only then can this country truly make a significant impact on the world, commensurate with its size and history.

QUESTIONS &
ANSWERS

Happiness and Self-Love

Q: What is the difference between self-love and self-centredness?

A : A strong sense of self is necessary to develop determination and willpower.

My favorite prayer is—"So long as space remains, so long as suffering remains, I will remain in order to serve them."

In order to develop courage, you need to have a strong sense of self. You need self-love. It's very necessary in order to have compassion for others.

In order to combat a self-centred negative attitude, you need self-confidence.

"SELF-LOVE

IS VERY NECESSARY

IN ORDER TO HAVE

COMPASSION FOR OTHERS."

The sense of self combined with ignorance and short-sightedness is wrong,
and this is self-centeredness.

Happiness and Compassion

Q: You talk a lot about compassion and happiness. If I am compassionate but someone I love dearly is in pain, how can I be happy?

"HOW DO WE BALANCE

CONCERN FOR ONESELF

AND COMPASSION

FOR THE WHOLE OF

HUMANITY?"

A: A great, ancient Indian master of Buddhism once raised this question.

Nobody wants pain, but if you practice compassion effectively, you will feel disturbed only for a short period of time when you find someone ill or going through a painful experience.

In such situations, your mental pain overwhelms you and you feel helpless because it hasn't come about voluntarily.

An excessive sense of concern for others' well-being causes discomfort. This happens voluntarily. You should try to develop that sense of responsibility.

Your self-confidence will give you the courage to care for another person's well-being.

A weak self cannot care for another being. Concern for others can spread to the whole of humanity. To all living beings.

Here is a story about this relationship—concern for oneself and compassion for the whole of humanity.

India has a very good culture of vegetarianism. In the early sixties, when I was passing through Dharamsala on the way to the Jammu airport, chicken could not be bought anywhere. Nowadays, every small restaurant serves chicken dishes in the name of progress. In Bengaluru, too, I noticed chicken being served with vegetables.

People consider chicken to be like vegetables. There is no feeling for the pain of the animal. In the summers, when it's very hot, the chickens sit shrivelled up in their cages, likewise in winters. It's very sad.

Of course, I am a nonvegetarian. I have reasons. I gave up meat in 1965 and was a strict vegetarian for a couple of months. During that period, following the advice of my Indian friend, I ate a lot of nuts. The result was that in 1966, I developed a gallbladder problem. Then I think for at least three, four weeks, I fell seriously ill and my whole body turned yellow.

At that time, I truly became a living Buddha—completely yellow. Not through spiritual practice but through illness. My doctors advised me to go back to my original diet.

"INNER STRENGTH BRINGS COMPASSION AND THIS ALLOWS YOU TO VOLUNTARILY TAKE ON OTHERS' PAIN."

So that's my story. We made all common kitchens in Tibetan monasteries completely vegetarian about ten or fifteen years ago.

When I was fourteen and in Tibet, I made all Tibetan government festivals vegetarian; they were traditionally nonvegetarian. Also, across our settlements in India, we do not have any kind of poultry, piggery, or fishery business. We are trying to promote vegetarianism. We need a worldwide movement.

About compassion—on the surface, you will be disturbed, but deep inside, you will get more self-confidence, inner strength, and voluntarily take on others' pain, and later you will get deeper satisfaction.

Happiness and Anger

Q: In our pursuit of happiness, we've heard about bad things like cruelty to our loved ones, cruelty to our neighbors, cruelty to animals; and in our lowest moments, such thoughts have haunted us.

How do we stop or delete such negative thoughts from our minds?

A : If you are angry, you will get mad; in anger we are frustrated and lash out, we might hit somethng or someone. But when you hit them, in the process your own hand might get hurt. Instead, be patient and compassionate.

On March 10, 2008, I had the same experience as that on March 10, 1959— helplessness, anxiety, and fear. But during the 2008 experience, I deliberately developed the practice of give and take.

As an example, I visualized the Chinese officials. I took their anger and

"PROMOTE AND CHERISH

POSITIVE EMOTIONS

TO GET RID OF THE

NEGATIVE THOUGHTS THAT

CAUSE YOU PAIN."

fear and gave my spirit of forgiveness and compassion to them. It brought me immense happiness.

It did not solve the problem of Chinese agression, but my mind was calm.

Anger destroys your peace of mind and eventually affects your health. Be compassionate and your mind will stay clear. Think along these lines, and you can develop full conviction.

I should not let anger or hatred disturb me. I must promote and cherish my positive emotions. Then comes the effort, which can take days, weeks, months, years, or decades. Then your mental state will change.

That much I can tell you through my own little experience.

Happiness and Illness

Q: Twenty years ago, I had asked you in Majorca what we should do as doctors when a patient is going to die.

But now I want to ask you what should a patient do to be happy when he is ill?

A : How we feel in illness depends on our attitude. If we believe in god, we will believe that we are creatures of god. God is all-knowing and infinitely loving, so our illness might have a meaning.

If you believe in the law of causality, you will feel that today's problems are the result of your past, negative karma.

Since karma is your own creation, if you create another, stronger, more positive karma, then the effect of the negative karma will reduce. So in some way, you will still have control.

For a nonbeliever, there's another way. Shantideva [8th century Buddhist scholar] had suggested that when you face a problem or have painful experiences, the situation should be analyzed.

If it can be overcome, there's no need to worry, because you can make an effort and take action to make change. If there's no way to overcome it, there's no need to worry either, because there is no action you can take to change the situation.

"TOO MUCH WORRY

IS SELF TORTURE.

EITHER YOU CAN TAKE ACTION

AND THERE IS NO NEED

FOR WORRY, . . .

. . . OR THERE IS NO ACTION

UNDER YOUR CONTROL,

AND THEREFORE

NO WORRY."

Too much worry is self-torture. It is better to not worry. This is not easy, but it is a realistic approach to face a problem.

More than ten years ago, I developed a painful intestinal problem. I was visiting in Bihar. I was passing through a village. I saw many poor children without shoes. In Patna, I saw an ailing old man on a bed, abandoned. In my hotel, I was in pain all night long, but in my mind, I could only see the children and the old man.

My mind was diverted to their misery out of a sense of karuna or compassion, and my own physical pain felt less severe.

Think more about others' well-being, then your own problem and sickness will feel less painful. Otherwise, I don't know.

Happiness and Politics

Q: I was wondering whether the request for not raising a political question comes from His Holiness or the organizers.

Politics does have an impact on our happiness in these times. Does justice form a constituent of the compassion you talk about?

"POLITICS DOES HAVE

AN IMPACT

ON OUR HAPPINESS

IN THESE TIMES."

A : Justice is at the level of action. Compassion is the motivation for action.

Compassion essentially means how to take care of others' well-being. So with that mental attitude there's no room for lying or deceit, no room to exploit or harm someone. You are taking care of their well-being.

There is also lying for the greater good. For example, Buddhist monastic practices mention that when a monk witnesses animals disappearing into the jungle and later lies to a hunter that he

"JUSTICE ARISES FROM COMPASSIONATE ACTION."

does not know about the animals, it is okay. A half-lie would be to say that he saw a bird go that way. That would be okay, too.

A lie is a physical, verbal action. Whether it's positive or negative depends upon our motivation.

I was once asked whether corruption was okay if the end result procured jobs for a large group of people.

This end result is from sincere, compassionate motivation! So here I would say *positive* corruption is okay.

So purpose and motivation are important. I have already retired from political responsibility. I voluntarily, happily, proudly handed it over to the elected political leadership, so if today anyone asks me a political question, I happily say that I've retired. So I have more freedom. If I want to answer, I do; otherwise, I say I've retired.

Happiness and God

Q: What is your definition of god, and how does one experience god?

A: I was once asked by a Westerner whether I'd seen Jesus Christ, and I said yes. I want to know what god is. It is a mystery.

Some things are beyond our thoughts; they are inconceivable. The Buddha was an enlightened human being of the highest level, someone beyond our thoughts.

Originally, he was just like us; step by step, he improved his mental state. That process we can study and understand logically.

Anyway, I think modern science can neither prove nor disprove god. It remains a mystery.

About the Author

His Holiness the fourteenth Dalai Lama, Tenzin Gyatso, is the spiritual and temporal leader of the Tibetan people. He has written a number of books on Buddhism and philosophy and has received many international awards, including the 1989 Nobel Peace Prize.

Titles in This Series

Be Happy

Be Angry

Be Here

Be Kind

Hampton Roads Publishing Company

. . . for the evolving human spirit

Hampton Roads Publishing Company
publishes books on a variety of subjects,
including spirituality, health, and other
related topics.

For a copy of our latest trade catalog, call
(978) 465-0504 or visit our distributor's
website at *www.redwheelweiser.com*. You
can also sign up for our newsletter and
special offers by going to
www.redwheelweiser.com/newsletter.